THE CANCER DIARIES

BOOK ONE:

FLOOD WARNING

W.F. LANTRY

FIRST EDITION

Little Red Tree Publishing, LLC

Layout and Cover Design: Michael Linnard
Text in Trajan Color, Minion Pro, and Arial.

First Edition, 2023, manufactured in USA
1 2 3 4 5 6 7 8 9 10   LSI   28   27   26   25   24   23

ISBN: 978-1-935656-67-8

Front and back cover photograph of Kate Landry was taken by W.F. Lantry.

Photographs on pages, 1, 4, 9, 10, 14, 17, 20, 25, 28, 33, 36, 41, 44, 49, 52, 57, 60, 65, 68, 73, 76, 81, 84, and 89, all by W.F. Lantry.

Comments in the "Word" section, at the front of this book, are published here by kind permission of the individual authors: Sandy Travis Bildahl, Patricia Prijatel, Maryann Corbett, Patricia Valdata, Claudia Piepenburg, Lala Corriere, Nadia Ibrashi, Sally Burdette, Margot Foley, Patience Mackarness, Sultana Raza, Linda Wastila, José Sotolongo, Joan Leotta, Christine Potter, Kathryn Bender, A'zam Obidov, Margot Brown, Jan Chronister, Susan Isla Tepper, Judy Kronenfeld, Hedy Sabbagh Habra, Hilma Wolitzer, Michael Sofranko, Craig Parker, James E. Lewis, Robert David Cohen, Yvette Wielhouwer Flis, Beth Benson, Wanda Lea Brayton, Charlotte Innes, Padmini Dutta Sharma, Tikulli Dogra, Clarence Major, Nancy Naomi Carlson, Alfred Corn.

Little Red Tree Publishing LLC
www.littleredtree.com

WORDS FOR
FLOOD WARNING

Words written from the corridors of the soul revealing a journey of joy, devotion, compassion and sorrow that allows us all to grieve, heal and rejoice in the truth that true love is possible.
—**Sandy Travis Bildahl**

I've been advocating for patients with triple-negative breast cancer for nearly 16 years, ever since my first diagnosis. I mainly talk to women who are diagnosed, but sometimes I hear from their loving husbands. I have never, however, heard a husband put words to this journey the way Bill Lantry has done. His poetry is pure, precise, true, and heartbreaking. We see Kate's diagnosis from his eyes, and we see his love. I think every woman who has gone through TNBC—and every man who has loved her—needs to read Bill's words. He touches our souls.
—**Patricia Prijatel**

In heartbroken honesty and flawless blank verse, these poems are a loving husband's account of the long trauma of his wife's cancer treatment. They might break your heart, too, but beautifully.
—Maryann Corbett

Bill Lantry's poems are filled with heartbreak and hope. A tribute to his wife's beauty and spirit, they chronicle the ordinary and the transcendent in exquisite detail. Whether Bill is in their garden or in a cancer center waiting room, he lets the reader into his heart. Every single word of these poems is written with love. It is a privilege to read this series of daily poems as each one is posted and to follow along with Bill and Kate as they negotiate such a difficult year.
—**Patricia Valdata**

Take this journey with Kate and those who love her and understand the transcendent beauty and strength and power of love...love against all odds.
—Claudia Piepenburg

Through the words of a poet, we glean a glimpse into a sad truth. There is no false promise here, and yet we enter a world of tranquillity, peace, and deep love. This is the reality Bill Lantry shares with us in his words and photographs of his beautiful wife, Kate, as they face the fate of her cancer together. In his photos, Bill captures Kate's majestic poise as she tells her own story. Behind her tender smile, you can hear her whispering words of joy. You can see the colors of glory only her eyes truly see.
—Lala Corriere

Bill Lantry delineates the quotidian pain at seeing his wife struggle with a serious illness. By alchemy, his words transmute into the highest art. He consoles himself with the most delicate musings about rivers merging, the poetry of Han-Shan, Hafiz, by the pond he designed and built, where lotus and koi coexist with joy. As winter approaches, he digs his garden hibiscus and places them in the greenhouse. Ultimately, Lantry's poetry is an ode to life and love.
—Nadia Ibrashi

Bill is truly a loving man to Kate, his family, friends, and the beauty in the world. He puts into words all the emotions of those who have been on this journey and all who are on this journey now. His poems bring insight, hope, and love to and for all.
—Sally Burdette

Kate, You are so lovely and loved by so many. You manage to smile even on your darkest days. I admire your strength and grace. Have faith that, given time, you will get through this, as I have. All I can do is send love, prayers and hope. Lean on Bill for strength and comfort; his words bring me both. Your sister warrior Margot in Bandon-by-the-Sea, Oregon.
—Margot Foley

I've never met Kate or Bill—we live on different continents—but some years ago when I had a story in Peacock Journal, I connected with Bill on Facebook. I've followed their story daily through Bill's poems and reminiscences, and the images accompanying them. Their beautiful garden. Kate's singing, Kate's face. Bill's words. Seasons, leaves, birds, prayer flags. Also the other stuff, the bad things that led to this sharing of so much that is beautiful.

The garden pictures bring something back that's stayed with me for years: in the Japanese Garden in Calderstones Park in Liverpool there is a deer-scarer, a bamboo tube that fills slowly with water, then tilts and releases a miniature cascade, before re-positioning itself and filling up all over again. A steady accumulation, then a pouring-out. I love it.

I'm grateful to Kate and Bill for sharing all this with a stranger, for letting me be a tiny part of what they're going through. For turning the conversation, always, to love.
—Patience Mackarness

These poems are heartfelt and probably written almost spontaneously, yet, the splashes of color or allusions to color make these images come alive. There's lots more to say about these poems... but for now, I'll only say that this genuine distilled outpouring of reflections and emotions in such a beautiful way resonates more with readers than very well-crafted poems revised many times that are too conscious of their own artfulness...
—Sultana Raza

Every day a new poem graces my Facebook feed, accompanied by photos: Kate and the glorious outdoors. I remember the one and only time I've met you both--at a reading in Baltimore to celebrate a PURE SLUSH publication. The gang was all there, all connected via fictionaut or 52/250, Bill outsized in chat and stature and Kate, quiet and powerful. Never in Bill's shadow. At the after-party we talked about our kids, how we worried about them, worried for them. I remember then I wished I lived closer to DC—I wanted to

be your friend. I wanted to keep talking about the important things: writing, gardens, and children.
—Linda Wastila

As I read these poems, I am reminded of bearing witness to the decline, and sometimes ultimate loss, of many I have loved. I can't turn the clock back and relive the times spent with them, but I look for little memories, segments of their voyage that I shared. Somehow, the details of these poems help with that search. They remind me of loved ones I saw through difficult times.

I wish I had recorded the specifics of what I witnessed—what they wore, what they said, when they slept, when they smiled. Those words would conjure their lives and I would rejoice in their being a part of me all over again.
—José Sotolongo

Bill Lantry's collection of six stanza three-line blank verse in iambic pentameter chronicles, with wife Kate's encouragement, the progression of her cancer and its treatment. This is a jewel of a collection of poems, one that rivals even the classic love poems. Dante and Keats, my two favorites, celebrate ideal women they never knew or who they never knew well. Lantry celebrates Kate who is his ideal but also very real beloved and his partner for more than a quarter of a century. This reality imparts an emotional depth to his work that even those great poets could not attain. With poems that are both empathetic and enlightening, Lantry reveals the couple's daily pain and hope, awkward moments, and the glorious times of simple pleasures in the garden, with their son, and stolen times of solitude when he as caregiver tries to recharge. These poems give readers a record, not of simply how to survive in a time of pain and suffering but also show us a way to overcome, to break out of disease's stranglehold through the power of love. He chronicles this in words and pictures, sometimes simply recording the grace and love of their daily lives including not only the treatments, the pain but also the daily acts of hope—walking in a garden, simply holding hands, watching the loved one as she sleeps. This is a book to keep by one's side, to read daily to learn the meaning of love.
—Joan Leotta

Every day, I do what writers and poets do: Cuss at Wordle, and then log on to Facebook to see who published where and to follow the feeds of a few poets who post daily or often. Ted Kooser does that, and I'm honored to be among the folks who get to see his new drafts. Bill Lantry does, too—although he has been doing it because he promised he'd follow his wife along with her cancer journey, a poem a day. The result is nothing less than stunning: the loveliness of the exotic plants he cares for in his garden, and the loveliness and strength of Kate, his wife, poem after poem. Especially considering they are new drafts, these are musical and vivid. Bill's love for Kate is like the sun that makes his plants grow, and his project is radiant with it. These are love poems in the truest sense of the term.

—Christine Potter

I first knew Kate and Bill through working days at Catholic University, particularly when our office hosted the annual Pie Day event and Kate would add to the festivities by singing a beautiful song. Their love for each other, as well as their shared love of flowers, always has been apparent.

—Kathryn Bender

I saw your post today, your many posts and poems about Kate. I don't know a lot about both of you, but I know you keep becoming a great supporting shoulder for her! Indeed, you are like a giant sycamore! We too have sycamores in sunny Uzbekistan and I love them. With a leaf of a sycamore here I would like to send both of you best of luck in your journey! Light to your life, strong health, good inspiration and prosperity!

—A'zam Obidov

Bill's poetry achingly yet inspirationally documents Kate's and his shared journey through the horrific minefield of cancer. It nourishes my hunger for the normalcy of real love in all of its expressions and reasons. I feel sure that is true for many, many others, as well.

And yes, there are infinite lessons to be taken from the actual poems themselves. None of them are wasted. We grieve and rejoice with

Bill as he shares his most intimate thoughts and moments with Kate through all of this.
—Margot Brown

A few years ago you were kind enough to feature some of my poems in Peacock Journal. I began following you on FB and could not turn away from your poems about your journey with cancer. Each one is skillfully crafted and pulls me in. The connection to your garden and pond speaks to me as a fellow gardener. Each new poem amazes me. The sharing of your experience can only uplift and strengthen anyone who embarks on the same journey.
—Jan Chronister

A solitude always hovers over these poems, during this most tumultuous journey into uncharted waters, not knowing if your jib will go slack, this solitude that rises from the deep ground and reflects back all of nature as we wish it to be, and hope it will blossom once again for darling Kate and Bill.
—Susan Isla Tepper

I don't know Bill (except as editor of *The Peacock Journal*) or Kate personally. But, as someone who has experienced cancer, and as a poet, I have loved reading these quiet, soothingly metrical and meditative poems tracking the natural world in the poet's garden, and beyond, and, with sorrow, hope, and such love, the cancer experience of his wife.
—Judy Kronenfeld

Bill and Kate's quest for beauty led them to create *Peacock Journal* and compile their contributors' musings on its meaning. Would beauty exist if not shared? Through their love for each other and art they helped poet friends transcend their limitations. I remember how peacock feathers adorned their AWP booths graced by Kate's elegance and beautiful smile. Bill and Kate's love for beauty is shown in their care for an idyllic garden and pond, in the way their camera captures every budding flower rivaling Kate's color-coordinated outfits in a constant renewal that defies the passing of time. Beauty exudes from every word of Bill's lyrical chronicle, which is a love letter to Kate

during her arduous journey toward recovery. Your love will be the healing secret that will get you all through these hard times.
—**Hedy Sabbagh Habra**

I just wanted to say I'm in awe of what you're doing. It takes a kind of wizardry and a great heart to make such beautiful art from hard life. I wish you and Kate the very best.
—**Hilma Wolitzer**

I just want to tell you how deeply your posts about Kate touch and move me. As someone who went through short-term—6 weeks—radiation and intermittent chemo, your enduring love for her brings tears to my eyes. I went through it alone. I would have given anything for the constant presence of love that you bring to her life. I admire you for this, Bill. You are a blessed couple. Keep on.
—**Michael Sofranko**

The first time I met Kate was in Bill's office in the Center for Planning and Information Technology at Catholic University. There were always several undergraduate and graduate student employees or interns in that area, lots of young people working with Bill's guidance to provide technical support to faculty trying to integrate use of computers into their teaching.

But Kate clearly stood out. A more mature personality; hands down, much better dressed; a quick smile; bright and cultured; and sophisticated, so that I wondered as the weeks went by and we saw more and more of Kate whether Bill had met his match.

And then there was her singing. I'm not sure when I first heard Kate sing, perhaps at one of the occasional social events we'd host in "the legal office," upstairs in the same building as Bill. One such event was a birthday party for the University President Father O'Connell, and Kate sang "Happy Birthday" in true operatic style, much to the delight of Father O'Connell.

My initial suspicions proved out, and my wife Betsy and I were privileged to stand up for Bill and Kate at their wedding a few

years later, presided over by their friend Father Bob Schlageter, in St. Vincent's Chapel at the university. And there I formed another lasting impression of Kate's enormous talent and spirit, which she generously shared as she sang at the wedding for her family and friends assembled there. That spirit still shines through in everything she does, whether raising their children or supporting Bill in his writing or in his ceaseless creativity in their gardens.
—Craig Parker

I've been following your poems on Facebook, and just wanted to let you know that you and Kate have remained in my daily prayers. Cancer has been too present in my family—mother, sister, now my oldest son. Much of what you are going through is familiar, even though it's personal to you. God bless both of you with strength and courage.
—James E. Lewis

I am wishing Kate and you the best possible outcome, a new cancer-free, healthy and happy chapter. Thank you for chronicling so deeply and caringly this intimate but universal human drama. Your love and your singing for Kate are so moving.
—Robert David Cohen

Honestly, yesterday, after I read the day's poem, moved, again, to tears at the beauty, the sensitivity, the openness, I thought how perfect might a book be, of the poems, chronologically, of this. Now you propose it. I feel like screaming "YES!" loudly, with emphasis on every hidden meaning, every silent fear and thought. But I don't want to shock anyone. So, yes. Please. I think it would mean so much. I think it would be impactful.
—Yvette Wielhouwer Flis

I think these words assembled are the true living love songs of good partnering in the ways of a diagnosed march toward an accompanied end of ends ending up roiling on the seas of all love in endlessness. Yours is a good guidebook for anyone wanting to accompany their beloved with the courage emboldened by your written truth. Please do as your beloved wishes for all your days together here in this whirling world. If ever there is this chance for

me to fall so deeply into the pool the two of you are in together—
well, let me dive headfirst into this endless love.
—Beth Benson

Your turning towards quietude and her holding the moment are
victories, indeed. The greatest success, the reason we're here, is love.
To learn how to give it, to learn how to accept it. It's the only thing
we may take with us when we go, and the only thing we may leave
behind, our greatest legacy of all. Your poems are like psalms, and
her obvious grace in photos is revelatory. A thousand paper cranes
with a thousand prayers are adrift within these tides of life. You
both have my sympathy and admiration. Your incredible poems, as
well as the obvious adoration and admiration for your beloved, are
stunning. I've been widowed twice, and have lost so many others
over the years, much too close together, and this is so deeply true
and profound. I finally realized that I couldn't experience such loss
had there not first been miraculous gain. The very notion that we're
on this rock, drifting through space, and suddenly, we're looking
straight into the eyes, heart and soul of love. I don't believe in
coincidence. You were meant to be together, and you were meant
to write these words of knowing/unknowing, to paint her in every
glorious shade of love. To share the journey, however long it may be,
is an honor and a privilege.
—Wanda Lea Brayton

These are powerful poems and they are well-made poems. The
careful detailing of it all—that's what makes them leap from the
page, along with the sense of profound suffering and the discovery
of beauty along the way. Suffering and beauty, and no sentimentality.
That's hard to do, and he does it so well.
—Charlotte Innes

Your writings are like sketches, I can see everything so vividly…
can feel the excruciating trauma you are going through … and that
is why my respect for you grows manifold as you give light and life
to Kate who needs you the most… you are an inspiration Bill… my
deepest regard for you.
—Padmini Dutta Sharma

On a rough day one look at Kate's kind, radiant face, the Zen like beauty of their garden, Bill's simple yet poignant poems washes away all the negativity from within. That's the therapeutic impact they have and then in their most adverse circumstances he found strength & courage to chronicle their journey through Kate's Cancer diagnosis & treatment. Each poem is a beacon of love and light not just for those fighting this dreaded disease, but also for caregivers, partners coping and assisting their loved ones through it.

For those of us searching for solace, Bill's words act as a soothing balm. The profound beauty in suffering, the fragility of everyday living, the reinventing of self despite all. It's incredible how he's woven it all in this delicate tapestry of words.

Bill's word imagery is incredibly moving. A world emerges as one reads his words & for that moment everything else fades away. The poems, luminous & deeply heartfelt, bring an order to the chaos.

I feel this compilation, deeply personal yet universal, will bring the warmth of love to those going through this illness alone and will become a companion they can reach out to at any given time. I'm glad these poems are being compiled into a book. Like Kintsugi it will fill the cracks with hope, love and reassurance.
—Tikulli Dogra

There is brilliance and wisdom here. Lantry has embraced a difficult subject—one loaded with pain, wonderment, and moments of pure joy. They are deeply felt, inspired, and skillfully constructed. They will endure.
—Clarence Major

I've found there's no better antidote to pain than writing it. Writing through it. When the body betrays us and spins out of control, we need something to hold onto. Some turn to faith and let doctors decide their fate. Others (like me) obsessively research all options until they reach a point where they realize they know all they will ever be able to know, and then must make life-or-death decisions based on what is often incomplete knowledge. It's nearly impossible to put aside all those emotions, kicking and screaming to be heard--including hope--in order to focus on living each day.

Writing did this for me. Writing does this for Bill Lantry. And what better vessel to express these feelings than in these controlled and beautiful 18-lined poems, all written in iambic pentameter, the rhythm of breath. No sentimentality lurks in these poems. Some of the most powerful emotions are expressed by not being stated, including the most important one of all—love. Bill and Kate's love will survive, as long as there are words.
—**Nancy Naomi Carlson**

Love makes itself known even (or especially) in hard times. It flows out from Bill Lantry's Kate in the garden settings where he photographs her and gives a parallel verse text for the image. What better representation of love can there be when it is enacted on the knife blade of a grave diagnosis? Art cares and it cures.
—**Alfred Corn**

CONTENTS

INTRODUCTION

I spend my days wandering around the garden with no real plan in mind: gazing at flowers, tying up vines, uprooting the occasional weed: such is the peaceful life of a humble gardener poet. It's a small garden, as such things go, but still, there are so many things needing attention any rational person would be overwhelmed when faced with today's list. So I simply walk along one of the garden's paths, and try to address whatever I find. There's a kind of freedom in unplanned action, the joy of wandering through a daze among the blossoms.

It was mid-afternoon, and I was near the lotus pond when the phone rang. It was Kate, my wife, known to her family as Kathy, known to the musical world as Kathleen Fitzpatrick. But poets and writers know her as Kate, and she is deeply loved by the community, for good reason, both here and abroad. Fifteen years ago she came to me, at the height of my professional career, and said "What are you doing? You're wasting your life. You haven't written anything in years. I want you to write one thing each day, a poem or a story, anything, and I'll send them out to be published. You're not allowed to come home for dinner until you've sent me something."

The results were, to say the least, surprising. Publications, books, prizes, awards, all due to her. When we did interviews, people didn't ask me many questions, they were far more interested in hearing from her. When we did poetry conferences, she'd hang back for the first couple minutes, and then she'd be out there, center stage, holding forth to a rapt audience, answering every inquiry and pointing out the direction for our journal, her journal: Peacock Journal. And it's not even her field, she's a coloratura soprano, with a voice that could melt all your resistance, pull back the veil, and open a portal to a timeless world of beauty and grace. Everything I've written since we met is a tribute to her. People, famous writers, would actually raise their hands and ask "Do you have a sister? I need a clone of you!" But medical science hasn't advanced that far, and she has no sisters: there's only one Kate, and though she may seem like a figure from an elegant dream vision, "she is mortal, and by the grace of providence she's mine."

So there I was, by the lotus pond, taking a break and watching the koi moving in their endless figure eights beneath the surface, when I answered the phone and heard her voice. If you must know, I love her voice so much sometimes I just listen just to listen. I am the most fortunate of men. But this time her voice was different, and it reached through the pleasant haze of my wanderings and woke me up. I actually asked myself 'What is she saying?'

She was saying she was at the gynecologist, and he'd found something, on the same side, and he was recommending a biopsy. Suddenly, I was completely awake. The same side? Twenty years ago, only a few weeks after we started dating, she found a lump in her breast. She had no idea how long it had been there, at the time she said she only found it because of my touch. Still just dating, we went through a whole series of medical visits, then surgery, then radiation. I tried to be there with her at every step, at every appointment. Even though we were nothing official to each other, I already loved her, as you may well have guessed, and anyway, no-one should have to go through such things alone. Five years later, I wrote this poem about those times:

Five Years

Before the discrete markings in her skin
could let well-tuned machines triangulate
the radiation beamed into her breast,
before the chemicals and all the drugs,
before the morning visit could divide
her life as previous or subsequent,

I drove her, with no rights, one afternoon
and walked her in. The nurses made me wait,
so all I have is second hand. It seems
at first the anesthetic didn't take.
She said "Is it supposed to hurt?" Their eyes
in panic told her no. Another shot

and then the knife went in. The miracle
came when they asked her what she did. "I sing."
"Sing us a song then…" As the knife explored
deep past the lymph, into her flesh, she sang
Lost Annachie, the first tune she had sung
to me, one afternoon, forgetting all

the words, which I supplied between the chords.
I was not there to give them, but she sang
what she remembered as they brought her out.
I held her then just as I hold her now
and each day, still, I notice those tattoos
between her breasts, and relish every breath.

The doctor told her at the time that while there's no good kind of
breast cancer, her's was maybe the best kind to have. Slow growing,
not terribly invasive. The surgery was successful. Nobody talks
about cures when breast cancer is involved, instead they say they
can find NED, "No Evidence of Disease." She chose post-surgical
radiation over chemotherapy because, as she told her doctor, 'I may
want to have a child with the man who will be my husband soon.'
She didn't tell me that, she only told her doctor. She always plays her
cards close to her vest. Everything about her is subtle and delicate.

And so we put all that in our rear view mirror. A year later we were
married, and then our son James was born. She wanted a house
so we bought one, she wanted a center hall colonial. OK, and I
want a garden. A real, permanent garden. I had spent many years
as a university professor, I'd taught at twelve universities on two
continents, and everywhere I went I made a garden, and when I
moved on to the next post, every one of those gardens was turned

back into lawn. But I'd left the classroom, and taken a position as Director of Academic Technology at a research university, and I had reason to hope for a garden with greater permanence. Alas, there was a housing boom, and the only house we could afford was a rundown three-story outside the beltway. It needed a lot of work. As soon as we moved in, I commandeered the garage, and turned it into a wood shop so I could work on the renovations. The garden would have to wait.

It waited a long time. James started school. Both my parents passed away, one from cancer. And her mother, also from cancer. And my oldest brother. The university restructured, and I found myself in early retirement. She was still singing, to audiences of hundreds, even thousands, every weekend. It was her calling, and she loved it. Then Covid arrived.

We figured James brought it home from high school. It was February, 2020. I caught it first, and it was not good. My doctor's office refused to see me, and suggested I go straight to the hospital. The hospital had no desire to see a potential Covid patient walk through the door. So I stayed in bed for ten days, sicker than I've ever been. Kate and James both had mild cases. I never really got better, and ended up in the hospital that summer, with what people now call long Covid. No-one was using that phrase at the time.

Having faced all that, in September I recalled my garden plans, and decided to build a greenhouse. I was still sick: many days it was all I could do to sit in the site I'd started clearing. But I was determined. In the midst of the pandemic, lumber was hard to find, all kinds of materials were hard to find. I sat out there, and some days managed to pick up a hammer, or a saw. September passed, and then October. The work seemed to strengthen me. By November, the frame was up. In December, I got it closed in.

She was Director of Music in a church. Covid closed the church. She decided she wanted to go back to teaching, and started working on that. I was building the garden: raised beds, fences, gates, ponds. One pond in the greenhouse. A small pond on the slope overlooking the Anacostia river. And the big pond, the lotus pond, at the center of the garden.

That's where I was when the phone call came. And a week later, when the biopsy results came back, she sat me down and made a serious request. "I want you to go back to writing a poem every day. I want you to document this cancer journey. I want you to write about exactly what happens, as accurately as you can. Don't leave anything out."

I told her I had Covid fog, and could barely think, much less write. I told her I didn't have that kind of energy. She said, "If I can face all this again, you can write a few poems." I told her I would.

I didn't do it simply because she asked, although that would have been enough. I had lost some old friends recently, one an editor, the other a poet. It's a strange phenomenon: people will be writing things, doing things, and posting online about them, and then imperceptibly the posts would drop off. But with so much happening it's hard to notice the absence of things, to hear silence amid all the noise. And these two women made a choice so many do: they didn't talk about their cancer diagnosis. They didn't tell their friends. They stopped communicating with everyone, withdrew into themselves, and then disappeared into the silence. Most of us only found out when someone forwarded their obituaries.

I didn't want that for Kate. She was not going to go gentle into the night, or quietly. She wasn't going to just disappear. That was my first motivation. We all want permanence. These are my favorite lines from *Ovid*:

> Give me yourself as matter for my song:
> The songs will come back worthy of their cause.
> Europa, Io, Leda live as long
> As we keep reading poets with applause.
> So may our legend last while verse endures
> And all that time my name be linked with yours.

Later, there would be other motivations. I hadn't yet heard the phrase 'tell your story of how you overcame everything, and it will become someone else's survival guide.' I didn't know how much these poems would mean to others as I posted them, day by day. Women who had gone through similar trials, spouses who loved them, family members who had lost their mothers, daughters, wives. As time went on, new people wrote me, people who had been newly diagnosed, and who were terrified, but they said that if Kate could go through this, so could they, and her story gave them courage to face what had to be done. But I didn't know that then. All I knew was that she was sick. And she asked me to do something. And I promised to do it.

But I didn't start right away. It was actually a few days later. I had already taken over the household duties, including the cooking. A stormy Friday evening. She was exhausted, sleeping upstairs before dinner. James was in his room. I was in the kitchen, starting dinner when I heard the flood warning on the radio. Four inches of rain predicted. I looked out the kitchen window, trying to see through the darkness whether the river was already rising. And I was overcome by a strange emotion, something I'd never felt before. So I turned off the stove, and walked upstairs, and wrote the first poem. And I called it Flood Warning.

W.F. Lantry
Washington D.C. 2023

FLOOD
WARNING

Flood Warning

A quiet evening. Dark. And rain outside—
They say we'll get four inches before dawn.
I'm in the kitchen while she sleeps upstairs.

Another day of biopsies, x-rays,
of ultrasounds and needles for the pain:
she's not supposed to pick up anything.

I'm cooking, listening to Keren Ann
whose voice reminds of Paris in the Spring
how many years ago in rain like this:

"The only things I still know how to make
are water ripples on the waveless Seine."
And me? I'm making rice and eggs. Young James

still has an appetite, and needs to eat.
Outside, the rain keeps falling, and the wind
moves through the leafless trees of early Spring.

I stand and stare at nothing, at the wind.
I cannot see into this foreign dark
where songs and shadows merge with endless rain.

April 21. 2022

Gold

She takes off all her jewelry: first a ring
acquired from her mother years ago,
another from her son on her right hand—

she loves them both. They easily come off.
Next come the bangles: one of corded gold
braided in Grecian patterns without clasps

another, mirror finished, with a dent
of unknown origins, reflective still
of everything around her in small spheres.

No metal is allowed in the machine.
Off comes her pearl necklace. Then she hands
each piece to me. I place them in a round

container with a lid and close it tight
swearing to guard it till the test is done:
there's fifty thousand dollars in that box.

And yet she can't remove her wedding ring.
The nurse says not to worry. She goes in
and disappears behind the closing doors.

Daily Practice

Today I write. And yesterday I wrote.
Tomorrow I will write again, although
the subject grows more difficult each day,

just as the storm clouds gather. Now, outside
the garden waits in rain and wind, as if
Spring were delayed and Summer came at once:

tornadoes happen everywhere. I know.
Here in our river valley, thick with trees
protected by low hills, I'd thought us safe,

but weather changes. Nothing seems the same
and so I walk the morning fencelines, watch
for any new intrusions near the ponds

and shore up what I can against the wind
as if I could do anything to hold
the storm within my hands and keep us whole.

Yes, rivers rise and fall. Branches will break,
She'll sing. And I will write. Tomorrow. Now.
And every day until the storm is past.

Changling

A lazy weekend morning in full Spring
and she gets up, then disappears from view.
In other times, she would return transformed

becoming who she'd want to be that day
or being someone private just for me
with all accoutrements soinly in place

six bangles, pearls, and a sapphire ring
resplendent in a skirt sewn with gold coins
or in a simple silken blouse undone

just so: a hint of elegance I love
in her, and all the lovers she becomes
each time I whisper stories in her ear.

But not today. She's in a faded gown
grey flannel, ankle-length, and unadorned.
Who is she now? She climbs back into bed

beneath the covers, with my big strong arms
encircling her, here in this quiet place
where she can be my good girl, warm and safe.

Intro to Statistics

They have a calculator on the web
The doctor asks us: "Do you want to see?"
You just key in your data: here – and here –

and it returns ten year survival rates.
It's triple negative breast cancer, so
you click this box. Drop down this history

for other cancers. Twenty years before?
And did you go for radiation then?
and surgery? Well, just click there, and now

move on to the next questions. Lymph nodes? Yes?
How many? Enter values in the field.
Have you been offered chemo? Then select

the proper dropdown for your therapy.
Enter your age and family history,
your general condition. Click submit.

It doesn't take much time to calculate:
the data set's complete and standardized.
We read the numbers printed on the screen.

April 28, 2022

Weather Report

I read the ten-day forecast constantly.
I heard whispers a couple weeks ago
of one cold night, beyond the frost limit

in late April. Most years, by now, it's warm
and there's no need for worry, but this time
something has changed. The forecast, transformed, fell

from forty, down to thirty-five, and then
to one night's frost. I watched it carefully
the way a gardener does, hoping for wind

since small currents can ease the chill effects
and we're along a river, so the air
flows down, on windless nights, above the stream.

But then, again, the forecast changed: two nights
no longer simply frost, but now a freeze
and then for three succeeding nights: too much

for tender April growth: Wisteria
blossoms are opening ephemeral
but this year more impermanent than most.

Rain

When lounging, half awake, with her beneath
the coverlets, entwined within my arms,
what good are calls to duty or devotion,

to the endless rhythm of the another day?
Better this peace, this harmony between
the morning darkness and the settled noon

now in April, when everything will grow
without me in the garden, reaching up
towards the gracious unencumbered wind?

It's best to rest this way and hear her breathe
feeling her heartbeat through her tender skin
and listen to her whispers. Minutes seem

eternal, counted only somewhere else
since here it may be yesterday or now,
it could be anywhere this music plays

this song of languor: our composed duet
more beautiful than any blossom held
above those vibrant leaves beneath the rain.

May 3, 2022

45 R 18

They called and said I should arrive at nine.
I made it at eight-fifty. It was cold,
the wind was blowing twenty miles per,

and I was in the building's shade without
even a coat to give a little warmth.
I didn't want to lose my place in line:

she would be waiting for me just at ten.
And I'd been anxious now for weeks about
that right rear tire, treadbare, gone to slick.

Each time she drove away, I worried, when
we went together to her rendevous
I wondered if we'd make it, knowing how

she'd worked to schedule each meeting time.
And so I stood inside that cold, and held
my place, because I—well, I needed to

and had to be on time to meet her in
the gardens for our daily morning walk
where blossoms waited for tomorrow's frost.

Late Frost

It should be Spring. New trees are blossoming
and I know all their names: the veined Dogwood,
bloodred Chestnuts along the riverbank,

and Carolina Silverbells paint wind
each time our breezes push them into waves
breaking against the base of southward hills.

And at their feet, small herbs are pushing through
almost like foam along a shoreline, blue
and silverwhite, swirling but motionless.

Climbing Hydrangeas cling to mortared bricks
and Clematis, rampant among bare twigs
open their leaves to our late April sun

But frost is coming. For three nights this week
late ice will cover petals, crystalline
and who can say what other winds will come?

I read the ten-day forecast hourly.
I should be planting, but my seedlings must
shelter within the greenhouse once again.

The Debate on the Joy of Fish

"Out swim the minnows, so free and easy. This is fish happiness."
~ **Zhuangzi**

She asked about my progress yesterday.
I mentioned how I'd raised the waterfall
nearly twelve inches in the greenhouse pond

and moved the pump down to the other end,
so now the filtered water gently flows
the whole pond's length, as if it were a stream,

to help the effervescent current bear
more oxygen, and how the golden koi
and all the fish seemed happier today.

"How do you know they're happier," she asked,
"you're not a fish, how can you know their mood?
And is there such a thing as happy fish?"

"I watch them carefully," was my reply.
I mark how they cavort within the foam,
describing caracoles with their long fins,

note how they rise to hand for bits of food
here as the water warms with coming spring,
until their joy transforms into my own!

Covid Fog

I'll write it later. Soon. There's always time:
the season isn't rushing on apace.
Our seedtimes last forever and a day,

The language isn't going anywhere.
My springtime mind is supple, stretching out
like branches reaching towards the other shore.

I know my subject and I know my thought,
the interplay of harmonies between
those two, and every crux to bind them fast.

And yet, just now, there's disarray and I
forgot to plug the car in overnight.
Three times in just one week. What came with ease

a year ago can barely be recalled,
not just the thing, but how it came to be.
The process of this mindful bricolage

is only half-remembered now and seems
a miracle of steady clarity,
unlike this fog obscuring everything.

May 8, 2022 - Mother's Day

Surrender Dorothy

I'd always wondered what it's like inside
that brilliant Castle near the beltway's curve
whose marble shimmers in the morning sun-

six gold-clad spires rising through the air
and one topped by the angel Moroni
whose trumpet calls the faithful to their prayers,

so Kate got tickets to their open house
after long renovations had repaired
an earthquake's damage. Lines like Disneyland's

snaked through a pristine tent, and then across
a walkway, without ornament, into
a welcome lobby. We asked questions there

of smiling greeters, who explained each stage
from basement bulls to the celestial
white space for hushed conclaves of elder men.

They kept their secrets hidden, as if Oz
called congregations to the upper floor
which held a thousand faithful unrevealed.

Last Frost

Hundreds of plants. Hundreds of plants inside
the greenhouse, on this last morning of frost
each sown from seed and raised for sixteen weeks

or more, and kept from winter under glass
nurtured, repotted, fertilized and trimmed.
Some forty trays with fifteen plants in each

on benches, on the ground, beside the door.
But as I bring them to the sunlight now,
each seems so small, and there is so much space

to fill: the garden's ready to receive
four times as many cuttings, seedlings, starts
of mostly rampant tropicals, whose blooms

will blaze all summer in this temperate sun
and then we'll need to do it all again
after the autumn frost cuts everything

to roots, at best, or like last winter's cold
to nothing, so I'll sow a thousand seeds
in preparation for the coming Spring.

May 9, 2022

Toll Road

We're driving north along I-95
she opens up her sewing bag, and takes
a dozen multicolored bobbins out

trying to match each to a bloodred scarf
whose faults I couldn't notice if I tried.
She settles on a single color, threads

one of a score of needles and takes up,
the cloth, the thread, the needle, all her work
regarding carefully the warp and weft

when suddenly we plunge beneath the bay –
there is no other way through Baltimore.
The tunnel's dark, except at intervals

where streetlights strobe the car's interior.
She's forced to set her work aside, to pause
and simply wait in contemplation here

beneath the harbor, underneath the waves
the ships, the gulls, the whole chaos of life
as we move through the darkness at great speed.

Aftermath

The front came through last night and dropped some rain
along with heavy thunder. Lightning. Wind.
The koi ponds overflowed. It's good for them

fresh water circulating in the clear
cleansed morning light now filled with Rachel's birds.
But Luna hates the thunder. She's a small

Australian Shepard, maybe twenty pounds,
and yet she has a beast of fear within
like all of us: a terror and a strength

we can't imagine on a windless day.
She ripped apart her crate—not just inside—
she bent black steel bars and tore up welds

contorted the whole frame and struggled out
then tried to hide. But there was nowhere safe:
She wept from room to room without relief.

Today with pliers snips and hammers I
repaired her broken crate as best I could
she watched in silence through the sliding doors.

Salix

Her grandmother, each year, at Eastertime
sent pussy willows from her garden as
a kind of greeting celebrating Spring.

She mentions it sometimes. So when I saw
those branches in the market, I brought home
a bundle of white catkins on long stems

she rearranged them in a crystal vase.
They last for weeks, although the catkins fall
and litter our blue tile with ivory.

I kept a couple stems aside to root
so we could have our own harvest next March.
They're in the greenhouse now recovering.

Willows will grow through anything—they'll send
new roots through water while still in their vase
and push out jade green stems whose slender leaves

reach out and up to catch the warming light.
I'll need to plant them as a living fence
against the rising waters of the stream.

Paradise

Mid-Spring, and yet the frosts are dangerous:
it nearly froze last night. A heavy dew
formed on the basil's leaves before our dawn.

The sun warmed everything by half-past eight
We met to take our daily exercise
walking through Brookside Gardens, near our home.

She asked me if I didn't need a coat
"Not if we're in the sun." And off we set.
It's often crowded, but this morning's cold

Kept most away. The paths seemed unadorned,
swept clean of every presence but our own
as if the earth were fashioned just for us:

The dawn redwoods now leafing out in jade
bright songbirds chorusing from hidden boughs
and cascades gently murmuring beneath

the accidental shade of bamboo groves
whose secrets are revealed as we pass
in conversation through the rustic gates.

May 13, 2022

The Art of Cooking

Fleurettes de broccoli and flaxseed oil
or mushrooms—better call them champignons,
much of her universe is French cuisine

as you would well imagine if you saw
the way she dressed for morning's promenade.
My research yesterday was diet, so

at noon I went to market, and brought home
armfuls of everything I read about:
tomatoes, tumeric, and haricots.

Her doctor messaged us this afternoon:
the recette of her chemotherapy.
Tonight I made her salmon bathed in herbs—

herbes de provence—garlic and olive oil,
I whisked in juice of half a lemon, cut
and placed a lemon slice on each filet.

I'm learning as I go. I guess we all
are learning things we hardly understand
in languages we almost thought we knew.

No Mow May

The garden's been neglected, and the lawn
is three feet tall—well, almost. Gone to seed.
It's No-Mow May in England after all!

I haven't trimmed the ornamental grass
or pruned the walnut limbs that overhang
the western fence where honeysuckle spreads

its tendrils out across last summer's mulch.
The mint needs weeding, and the bee balm flows
beyond its limits in the grand design.

There's just no time. The season's run away,
and what was critical three weeks ago
seems almost meaningless. I had such plans

and still hold each plan close: the Torii gate,
the eastern lantern made of fait-main stone,
a whole new hedge line near the NorthWest path,

but even there wisteria has spread:
its untrimmed runners intertwine the fence
and even threaten jade stems of bamboo.

May 19, 2022

Climate Change

I've seen a quarter century of Mays
here in zone seven—once predictable,
our planting dates are changing by the year

I still remember—almost—every one
in flood or flame, cold wind or early June's
sweltry arrival, three weeks early, dry.

I'd thought I'd learned to plan the season out
imagining the garden in full bloom
and counted backwards twelve weeks from last frost

This wind surprised me. Now, I cannot guess
what other Mays will look like—will there be
the kind of blossoms every almanac

assures us will return, just now, each year
or will there be a garden here at all?
I cannot say. I only know these hands

are used to planting. There's a kind of joy
in seeding, staking, shoring up the earth
and co-creating paradise each Spring.

Watercolors

We walk through Brookside Gardens every day
at ten o'clock. I offer her my arm
and off we go into the vibrant woods

on cloistered rainy blossom-bordered paths
while voices in the trees are chorusing
the promised sweet songs of an endless Spring.

Last night she had a nightmare. In her dream
creatures surrounded her. She lost control
then called my name, awoke, and came to me.

We single file cross a narrow bridge
there is no rail, and the polished stone
is slick with rain. She reaches back her hand

I take it, and we go together through
a rustic unlocked gate. Two Springs from now
will I be helping her regain her strength

or will I have to help her leave this life?
Those birds, continuing their endless song
color the air with iridescent notes.

Taxi Driver

Because she couldn't make it on her own—
not if she had to do her whole commute—
I pick her up at twenty after twelve

and tell the car to head towards Baltimore.
She's radiant—a silken iris scarf
stringed pearls and a silver pleated skirt—

the contrast of her elegance with my
rough nature has sustained me twenty years:
the Californian and the East Coast girl

rolling together now across the earth.
She's on her phone attempting to arrange
another test her doctor specified

an ultrasound, more x-rays, or perhaps
a morning measure of her cortisol—
the challenges become logistical

and she excels at those: she will persist
until each intervention is arranged
and hasn't reached the stage of letting go.

The Kitchen Debate

Two months ago I'd listen to her day
or sit across the island and read out
whatever story seemed to interest her

but I'm the one who cooks the dinners now.
I built this kitchen from her own design
the island, counters, cabinets, everything

just as she drew them up and laid them out.
She didn't like the first version, so I
ripped out the walls and did it all again.

Tonight she sits across the island as
I ask for her advice while setting up
the pots and knives, spices and vegetables.

"Don't use that pan," she says, "and that old scale
is unreliable—get out the new
it's near the oven cupboard, standing up."

It's hard for her, this letting go of space
seems almost like a letting go of all
she's held so close for nearly twenty years.

May 20, 2022

Emploi du Temps

Wake up, and take young James to Springbrook High
come home. You have a little time before
the telemedical oncologist

take in her news: you have to leave some space
to let it all become reality
but only in your mind: no time for that

you have to pick Kate up right after twelve
then it's a new race to Columbia:
her ultrasound appointment's before one.

Get done, race back—they say a thunderstorm
may spawn a few tornadoes around two.
You must be back in time to pick up James

around two thirty. Get Kate back to work,
go straight to James' school and bring him home
in time for his own telemedical

appointment around four. Log into yours
at five, and find some time amid all this
to comfort her, and hold her close and safe.

Technicolor

I'm used to ultrasounds: with all those boys
I've seen a few. But they're in color now:
The passages of blood flash red and blue

Depending on direction of their flow.
Kate's buoyant, and she's making little jokes
'You see, Darling, I have a beating heart

so I'm a real girl after all.
It isn't even broken!" We can see
the rhythmic evidence up on the screen:

the valves open and close in real time
blood moves in cadences. Her nurse points out
tricuspid valve regurgitation on

the technicolor screen. "It's not acute,
don't worry. There is no significant
valvular dysfunction." We're relieved,

we just came for a baseline after all.
But something shifted in me as I watched
as if my heart should beat in place of hers.

May 23, 2022

Ram Dass Was Right

Stop thinking William. Stop considering
the possibilities of everything:
There's just here, now. That dandelion root

needs to be plucked before it goes to seed
reach down and pull it out. Pick up a leaf
of lemon balm and rub it on your skin

it smells so fresh. It smells of vibrant life.
Some early strawberries are turning ripe
reach down and take one. Savor the deep red

savor the form and taste and the delight
you feel standing here among the trees
surrounded by birdsong and beating wings

surrounded by the blossom-scented breeze
warmed by the midmay sun. Stop thinking. Watch
the way the surface ripples of the pond

move through the circled water lily leaves
see how the koi are gliding underneath
the mirrored surface of the lotus pond.

Heat Dome

It started out near Abilene last week
we barely noticed. But the warming spread
first south to Austin and the hill country—

I know it well: the rocks and rattlesnakes
would be alive with motion in that heat
beneath the ragged shade of small scrub oaks—

and then expanding up through the great plains
to the north country: pheasants prairie wheat
all withered. Moving east, high pressure spread

the warmth to Memphis, Nashville, Lexington
and on to us: today, ninety degrees
tomorrow afternoon to ninety-eight.

I know in other places it's the same
in India and Spain there's suffering
and even worse than here. It's only May.

I know this summer will be difficult
and all of us must gather our strength now
anticipating savage thunderstorms.

À bout de souffle (Breathless)

Stay strong, William. There are so many songs
and this one now is yours. Six months ago
long covid had you ready to withdraw

but that was just a luxury. And now?
Although you can't go up a flight of stairs
without losing your breath you must go on.

You're sixty-five with cardiac disease
two arteries half blocked, and overweight,
arthritic shoulders and some squamous cells.

So what? Young James is only seventeen
and needs you steady. Lift those barbelled weights
harden your shoulders and refresh your heart.

But mostly work your core: you'll need the strength
to carry her both up and down those stairs.
So when you reach their landing, do not pause

to catch your breath. That's just indulgence. Sing
the song you're given with the voice you have
for him, for her, for everyone who hears.

Chip Drop

You cannot know exactly when they'll come
or what they'll bring: sometimes you'll get a text
or you'll return to find the driveway blocked

when you come home exhausted from a day
of blood draws, ultrasounds, or just more news:
there's always more. There's always more to do,

and gardens need a plenitude of mulch
now with the changing climate and the heat
turning to storms and washing down these slopes.

You'll ask for chips, but sometimes a few logs
get mixed in 'accidently,' and you'll need
to pry them out from underneath the heap.

You'll need to get the driveway cleared by dark.
Twelve yards makes up three hundred cubic feet.
Your cart will carry seven for each trip.

The garden fence is sixty yards away.
It's ninety-five degrees outside in shade.
Get up. There's much to do, William. Begin.

May 23, 2022

Lassitude

Three days of heat to warm our lily pond—
the water plants beside themselves with growth—
then after dark a three inch thunder rain.

Rainwater ran through everything, and touched
electric lines somehow—I still don't know—
I had to switch the power off outside.

It's true: each day plants give off oxygen
but take it back at night, and suffocate
whatever's in the water: tadpoles, fish,

the biggest one's always the first to go.
I found a ten inch white koi floating when
I went to check this morning after dawn.

I restarted the pumps but left him there
hoping he might recover. Now he's gone.
Scavenged? Or disappeared into the depths?

The water's all disturbed, and I can't know.
But I've no energy to drag the pond:
I sit and watch the surface full of hope.

Sleepless

She's having trouble sleeping: yesternight
I opened every window in her room
to cool all the house, but rainy wind

brought a new increase in humidity,
and then the birdsong kept her half awake
near dawn, so she was tired when we walked

after the rain had stopped just after ten.
She's often chatty, but we walked today
in peaceful quietude among the trees

the forest's dogwoods blooming pink and white,
or candelabra chestnuts blazing red
whenever sunlight slipped between the clouds.

She said "I'm scared of chemotherapy,"
coldcaps and IVs, ports and chemicals—
hours of treatment starting late this week.

Then we walked on in silence underneath
the canopy of trees that held us both
in contemplative hushed serenity.

May 25, 2022

Santa Rosa Labyrinth

We watched them work for weeks recutting stone:
the dryfit wall back-mortared to the slope
was finished yesterday. We stopped, and heard

a smiling foreman pointing out the new
stone features of our favorite labyrinth:
we've walked its ways so often these last years.

She always enters first, and I, behind
will pause a few moments to watch her go
then follow, contemplating how the curves

move us apart, across the symmetry
then guide us back together. When we meet
she stops, I take her in my arms, we kiss

and then the labyrinth pulls us apart
again. Sometimes, I reach my arm across
the spiraled space to touch her outstretched hand

but always, at the end, we meet inside
the central heart-space where, within my arms
her smile nearly blossoms in the sun.

Merlin

I downloaded a birding app today
so many singers hide among our trees
it hears their songs then shows me who they are

and gives a list of species: forty three
so far. Warblers, waxwings, and even hawks
the redtails of my western youth replaced

by sharpshinned, red shoulders, even ospreys
along the riverbank close by our house.
I'm moving backwards through my memories

remembering the birds we saw last week
or last year, walking through the forest when
she pointed out a heron near the stream.

Or on the seashore several years ago
watching the tiny shorebirds interweave
their patterns through the waves one afternoon

I see her standing there, her woven hat
casting bright patterns on her silk sarong.
I still don't know the names of those small birds.

What To Expect

It's her first chemotherapy today:
I need to pick her up at ten past nine.
I forgot her favorite hat. Well, never mind.

It's always rush to wait. There's a nice room
It's all drug pumps and monitors and tubes.
Go get her coffee. Grab some oreos.

The nurse takes her to slicken back her hair.
The cap reminds us both of Knute Rockne—
She looks like she could break a flying wedge

that might hurt less: she hates the sudden cold.
I get her extra blankets for the chill.
Keytruda goes in first. It makes her jump

They reset her IV and all is well.
I tried to build her up and make her strong
but now, between the coldcap and the drugs

she's suffering, and then she passes out.
I watch her sleeping, with a single wish:
To take her in my arms and make her well.

Fireflies

She's up! She's walking! She went off to sing!
Young James went out to share a birthday feast.
And I'm alone inside an empty house.

What can one do? Outside, the evening's calm
the garden needs attention. Strawberries
are ripening unnoticed in their bed

I gather up what's there and eat them fresh
their luscious pulpy mellow divine juice
drips from my hand and marks the sunset leaves.

Spring rains have washed away the greenhouse path
and left a soggy mess: remove the door,
build up the sill, and go look for more mulch.

The hillslope lawn, beneath the cherry trees
has come alive with fireflies at dusk.
They light my work as I fill up the cart

and light my path as I go down the slope
descending through the cherry boughs and pines
as swallows change to bats above my head.

May 30, 2022

Small Joys

Some poet friends wrote, asking after Kate
and asking for our address. I replied
and yesterday a smiling fedex man

came down the driveway bearing packages:
herb teas and chocolate cookies, turmeric
and other spices for her afternoon.

He seemed so happy. How could he have known?
Perhaps her face lit up with calm surprise?
And she was touched that others thought of her.

She christened them her cancer cookies, and
young James and I are not allowed to touch!
They're sitting on her dining table now.

She means to write back, if she has the strength
but she's in bed just now, half in repose
and half concerned with other pressing needs:

I bring her water every time I climb
the stairs. She does her best to drink it all,
small signs of struggle in her lovely eyes.

Into the Shade

Ninety degrees. Perhaps a little more
and not a single cloud above us as
we break the forest's cover into May's

cascades of sunlight over dogwood boughs:
rivers of luminescence rushing through
the waterfalls of scarlet chestnut trees

and pooling near the roots of cypresses.
We hurry down along the curving slope
back into dark along the river's edge.

She breaks the pathway unexpectedly
stepping from stone to stone within the flow
and I, trailing behind, offer my hand

each time she hesitates. Small polished stones
lead us upstream into the cooled air
and early summer's flowers light the way

until the gentle passage disappears
and we, reluctant, hesitating, pause
for one brief moment in the quiet shade.

June 4, 2022

Identity

It's silk or satin, cotton or bamboo?
And hats and scarves and pillowcases made
without stitches or seams? You wouldn't think

the complications could be infinite
but each decision leads to a new branch,
each branch into an unfamiliar wood

remote, exotic, inaccessible.
The cold cap treatment led to misery
no more of that, thank goodness. But her hair

the signal of her femininity
will disappear within the coming weeks.
She's mourning as I shop online for wigs.

Free? Or expensive? Real? Synthetic?
Headband? Full-headed? Sewn into a hat?
Would you like to be a curly headed blonde?

"I just want to be me," she said, and turned
into my arms. I held her as we looked
at all the choices, knowing there were none.

Second Session

It's quiet on the chemo ward today
quiet and dark. The thunderstorms outside
are sweeping from the south, bringing hard rain

at five o'clock. Inside, most folks are gone
we're now the only ones left in this hall
except for nurses, navigators, aides.

It's not as bad as last time. There's no cold
to trouble her repose. Her restless legs
are covered by three blankets. She still wants

to do things for herself, get up and move
dragging behind her the tall chemo tree
with four infusion pumps. I turn to close

the sliding chamber door. She tries to sit
but falls. I pick her up for the first time
since all this started, place her in the chair

and watch her as she falls back into sleep.
The first time's always hardest. From now on
I'll know to listen closer to her breath.

Knowing Ourselves

We think we're gods. Don't laugh. You know it's true:
we think we'll dance forever and a day
we can't believe we'll die and disappear.

We give lip service to mortality
but can't imagine nothingness. Our books
have just one theme: 'remember, you are dust

all is illusion, the ten thousand things
turn in their gyres without you: surrender.'
We don't believe them. Deep within our hearts,

we cannot leave our deep loves or ourselves.
'The world won't miss you' Heidegger once said,
'but you will miss you.' In the cancer ward

so many rooms encompass private lives
behind glass sliding doors. As things progress
the gaps grow smaller till the doors are closed.

We think we're gods. We know we give off light
and hope to bathe the luminescent Earth
like fireflies who dance until the dawn.

Dawn

It's almost magical outside that door
you'll notice blossoms first and then birdsong
surrounds you as you move across the deck

among hibiscus, roses, clematis
pause on the staircase landing fifteen feet
above the garden with its wreath of vines:

long tendrils brush your hands as you descend.
Watch dragonflies trace patterns on the wind
or land on lanterns and sculptures of cranes

check on the ponds whose water lilies spread
round leaves and blossoms on calm surfaces
look for wine cannas past the redwood gate

scan for new blossoms: yarrow, penstemon.
Deep at the garden's end bend down and pluck
some burgundy June-bearing strawberries.

She's sleeping still upstairs, recovering:
go out the door, take just a little time
to reinforce your spirit for the day.

June 8, 2022

A Body In Motion

She doesn't want to give up anything.
She's out today. Well, she has things to do:
she's shopping, seeing people, singing Mass.

She'll come home weary, like she did last night
needing to rest, exhausted, lying down.
I'd made a real dinner, but could see

she wasn't up to it, so I rewarmed
a little salmon from the night before.
She slept all night, and well into the day.

She couldn't bring herself to order wigs.
I went online and ordered a few things
Who knows what I got right? Headscarves and wraps

and bamboo caps for sleeping. When it starts
we'll need to have diverse materials
something to choose among, to give a sense

of actual control. Or so I've read.
She's racing. Well, eternity is hers:
she's running endlessly on restless feet.

Delicate

It's dawn outside, well, nearly: vireos
are moving through the understories, wrens
climb down tree trunks headfirst, awake, alive –

The earth's a quiet place, and delicate.
I'm waiting for young James to rouse himself.
Koi in the willow pond expect their food

and glide beneath the surface, red and white
against the sky's reflection where their fins
seem almost like the wings of butterflies

their arching dance almost a jeweled flight.
I find a tranquil joy along the edge:
twelve tiny newly hatched red minnows school

close by the parrot feather, where they're safe
and have a place to hide. What could I do
if something came for them? They're on their own.

I need to go inside and wake up James,
but spend a moment watching as they flit
between the spiral leaves into the dawn.

June 15, 2022

Wigs

She's recommended by the hospital:
Good wigs for chemo patients. Worth a try.
Her house is in a pleasant neighborhood

not far from ours: brick walls and shaded lawns
but there's a dumpster parked along the curb:
she's ripping out a deck and building new.

I started questioning once we walked in—
the front room seemed a shop for halloween
six dozen wigs on mannequin head stands

arranged by length and shade—straight, curled, waved?
She sits us down in her back room, and tries
a wig on Kate's head. Honestly, it's nice

and can be styled to our preferences.
She tries on a few others, but that one
Kate likes the best, until she asks the price:

"Five thousand dollars. It might last a year
or maybe less?" We thank her for her time,
and walk outside, speaking of hats and scarves.

Sweetness and Light

I curse myself for listening to songs
by Keren Ann or Coralie Clement:
their silken voices, supple, velvety

are all I seem to wish for these last days –
these little nothings we have loved so much
the mellow whispering of breezy words.

There was another time, when I believed
in edges, corners, twists and ragged turns,
spectacular displays of fireworks

caught in a centrifugal turn of phrase
the distilled essence of reality
captured and glistening in mirrored words.

No longer! Smooth the corners for me now!
I do not wish to burn in gemlike flames
or cut myself along the bleeding edge:

a few hairs on her pillow were enough
to change my mind this morning. Now I long
only for peace and blissful harmony.

Fury

Tuesday the weekly blood draw was complete
The nurse called Wednesday. Everything was fine:
the Thursday chemo session's set for three.

But Thursday morning someone called: a test
that should have been included on Tuesday
was missing from the clinic's orders, so

could we come in a little earlier?
We'll do the test and still proceed at three.
OK. So we get up there around one

they put in an I.V. and draw some blood
still saying all is well, and then at three
they guide us back into the chemo room.

We wait, and wait, and wait, and then at four
two nurses enter. Chemo's not prepared
a doctor hadn't called the pharmacy,

and now it's closed, there's no time, we should leave.
I want to scream. Kate almost wants to cry.
It's hard enough already. Then there's this.

Wearing the mask

Sirens and helicopters everywhere
a cloudy summer day in Baltimore—
graffiti on the walls as we drive past

Paul Laurence Dunbar High at Nine A.M.
The garage seems nearly empty and we park
close to the elevators, just in case.

This other building seems industrial:
a dozen patient beds arranged in pods
no rooms, just curtains to define our space.

Now settled into chemo quietude
the fierce woman I know begins to fade
she's like a young girl curled up in bed

who calls me Doc but seems to call me dad
though he's been gone for nearly forty years
and I'm a pale substitute who folds

the blanket awkwardly around her legs
turns off the lights, and sits in silent watch
disconsolate beside her narrow bed.

June 17, 2022

Chop and Drop

A deer got in the garden overnight
she must have entered sometime around dawn
the dogs were still asleep and derelict

as always, in their duty. She could browse
in peace through all the beds, just tasting this
or that: hibiscus tips? She nibbled three

before deciding there are better treats
a little farther up the hill, and left.
It means I need to fix the broken fence

where fallen limbs had knocked a section down.
It's hard to find the time. I need to prune
rank parrot feather near the water's edge

and use the trimmings as a kind of mulch
beneath the Angel Trumpet's spreading limbs.
They call this 'chop and drop': using the dead

to fortify the living. I should leave
the fence broken. Why not? All things must pass:
Hibiscus tips. Green parrot feather. Us.

The Paris Bird Market

Montmartre: a fifth floor loft—chambre de bonne—
all day a noisy ventilator fan
up from the rough trattoria below

consumed the space preventing even thought.
And so I built a nice expansive cage
and walked down to the quatrième. Back then

a bird market at Place Louis Lépine
offered small finches: orange cheeks and red ears
I bought four pairs and walked carefully home.

They built new nests as soon as they arrived
but mostly they would sing: their tiny chirps
broke up the ventilator noise and gave

a kind of cheerful peace, a sense of life
continuing in spite of everything.
I have some finches with me here. Just now

they're caring for three nestlings, and they're loud
their joyous songs distract from solemn thoughts:
I celebrate their careless revelry.

June 24, 2022

How Are You?

It almost doesn't matter how I am.
I'm not the one who's—well, no more of that.
You're sweet to ask. I'm trying not to weep:

it wouldn't do much good, and I have shed
enough tears for a year these last few weeks—
I'm not sure how much more I have inside.

I note a kind of heavy emptiness
where once creative waters overflowed.
There isn't energy for anything

except what must be done, as if the gods
set unexpected tasks for each of us,
and gave us just enough to move along

to stagger towards a distant finish line.
I think of marathoners turned around
confused, exhausted, still with far to go

determined to press on, refusing aid.
It's sweet of you to ask: I'm feeling fine—
ready to face whatever's still to come.

Age

I'm old. Baird's thirty. All my hairs are white
and they've been white for well on twenty years:
I said I'm old. My bones make noises now.

And yet, today, it's ninety-four degrees
and I was in the garden mending fence
tending three ponds, and planting out new starts.

OK: I have to pause after the stairs
but I can walk on level ground, and pull
a loaded cart across a mound of earth

so how old can I be? And how can time
the only thing we actually possess
be measured when we simply live for now,

as if the future becomes memory
by constant motion, moments flowing through
our lives like wind passing through my white hair?

My bone's ticking sounds like a second hand
on a blank watch as I descend the stairs
and open, once again, the garden's door.

Life List

She tires easily. Now, when we walk
she leans against me, gently, for support
and wordlessly convinces me to slow

each time we climb even a mild hill
so halfway up, we stop, and I point out
the blossoms of whatever plant is there

the leaves, the shadowed stems, just anything
to let her recollect herself before
the climb continues up towards the crest.

Or I will question whether those small birds
are on the list I started weeks ago
and pause to look them up. So far, we've reached

four dozen species just in this small place:
our garden, and this park one mile away
where Rachel Carson wrote her *Silent Spring*.

She leans against me, smiles, we move on
discussing birds and blossoms, wind and clouds
as we descend into the deepening shade.

Fourth Chemo

Phone, tablet, glasses, earpods. Do I need
her drugs, or will they have them for her there?
Should I put them in the back seat just in case

or would the summer sunlight ruin them?
The outside temperature is 102
according to the sensors on the car.

She's late. We should be driving there by now
but why be anxious? Hurried? In Dante
the souls clamor for entry into hell

but why should we be rushed? This afternoon
Keytruda carbo taxol benadryl:
it's not a dinner party. She'll pass out

and I will sit in silent watch for hours
arranging pre-warmed blankets on her legs
watching her restless sleep. Remember these

are the good days: she still has all her hair
her mind is clear. How long? No-one can know.
The drug pump's clicking measures passing time.

June 26, 2022

Sisterhood of the String of Pearls

Skirt Sisters of long standing wish her love,
unknown Pink Sisters give encouragement
and offer her stories of coming through

in spite of fear, in spite of all the pain
they call each other warriors and fight
the strange demon within: "You are not lost

and you are not alone. We have endured,
in your worst moments know you're one of us
and just as we've persisted, so will you."

But there is yet another kind of love
unknown to me till now. Someone will write
asking for our address, and then will send

some small gift: scarves or balm or herbal tea
a quiet comfort or a graceful joy.
Sometimes the cards are signed. The last one read

'The String of Pearls Sisterhood.' Her eyes
clouded a moment as she held with love
the gift of silk within her jeweled hands.

Father's Day

We've known for several weeks this day would come:
she's losing clumps of hair, and some of mine
is falling too! They say proximity

to chemo drugs can cause this: we were warned
not to be intimate, were told to sleep
perhaps in separate rooms, but I refused.

I now remember: twenty years ago
the only thing I wanted on this earth
was just to hold her in my arms, and so

the admonitions of a kindly nurse
seem meaningless: Kate lays her weary head
on my strong shoulder, and we close our eyes

at least for a few moments—there are things
we need to order: Irish headband wigs
silk pillowcases, bamboo scarves, paisley

bandanas, and we'll have to cut her hair
sometime this week completely off, she'll be
my sun-screened beauty in a summer hat!

June 30, 2022

Capybara

I understand the wish for miracles:
some spell, some charm, some magic token worn
around the neck or wrist, a quiet song

repeated as a ritual within
a darkened room, with incense: if I could
I'd cast a circle with the best of them

of salt or sand, I'd smolder the white sage
that grew in California near my home.
But I'm no witch. I'm just a mortal man.

A singer sent her capybara stew
and roasted capybara. She's polite:
she took a taste so she could say she did

and so her choir sent her more of both.
It's not crazy. Now, at the N.I.H.
they're studying the capybara's genes

but eating them won't help. Still, it's the wish
her choir members have to keep her well
that lets me store it on the kitchen shelf.

"O Mercy!" To Myself I Cried

She went into her surgery with rings
and bangles, but I took her pearls off
and placed them in a scarlet eyeglass case.

The smiling nurse told me to wait outside
I kissed her goodbye there. They rolled her out
along the hallway and through double doors

closing behind her, and then she was gone.
They say she won't remember anything.
But I'm still fully conscious with nowhere

to go, and there is nothing I can do
for hours as I wait. It's just a 'port
placement' I tell myself, it's just to ease

her chemo treatment, and replace IVs.
But I can't keep strange thoughts out of my mind
I try to reason with myself and lose.

I know another time like this will come,
I know there'll still be nothing I can do
except to sit in silence in this room.

In Search of Lost Time

She couldn't sleep this morning or last night
through hours up and down for different drugs
her skin's stretched tight around the I.V. port

swollen and red and painful. Nausea
on top of everything kept her awake
so now today she's tired, edgy, short.

It's hard to blame her: I would be the same
or worse, besides, there's no time to be cross:
we stop speaking a moment, then we leave

together for our walk a little late.
The park is nearly empty with this heat
and there's a storm watch, so we hasten on

not even pausing at the labyrinth
or weaving through the rose garden, the wind
comes up, and droplets ripple on the pond

but we can't hurry up the concrete stairs
and so the raindrops fall on both of us
until we reach the shelter of the car.

Dulce et Decorum Est

Enough reality. "Can I be done?"
she asks before the doctor makes it in,
"Can this be over now?" Well, not today,

It's June, we're only up to the fifth week.
And there are new procedures now: taxol
requires her to ice her hands and feet.

But there's good news, or absence of more bad:
the tumor's softer. That means it responds
to all this chemo, and those four lymph nodes

no longer palpable, have disappeared.
But each time this gets harder: more fatigue
more nausea, more pain, more everything.

If you could see her supine on the bed
by tubes connected to four chemo pumps
half-conscious, restless legs wrapped up in cloth,

my friend, you might be tempted to agree
to tell her yes, it's over, that's enough
and warm her hands and feet with your own flesh.

June 30, 2022

Pity and Terror

Some folks like roller coasters. Not for me,
it's just fake danger. I climbed Lembert Dome
without a rope: I know what terror is.

Some folks watch horror movies, slasher films,
or bloody gory battle epics set
in foreign places during distant times:

it's hard to understand. Philosophers
suggest we have within us violence
and wish to see it played out on the screen

as if watching could purge our deepest fears
as if horror could pave a path to peace
and so we seek the worst and rush right in.

For me it's posts by others going through
chemo and radiation, surgery.
Searching fine points and technicalities

searching for hopeful signs, but wondering
if I'm not watching gladiators bleed,
or riding roller coasters out of fear.

Hibou

For twenty years each summer night we've heard
a great horned owl call from the forest's edge
or somewhere distant near the river bank

but never saw it, although I've stood still
along the garden fenceline waiting for
some hint of movement among sycamores

or searched the dead branch snags in faint starlight.
I've even walked beneath the floodplain trees
looking for banded plumes I've never found.

Some think of owls as messengers, and some
believe they're furtive travelers between
our vibrant world and those darker shores

where wingbeats are the only hints of breath
and seeing one means sudden change is near.
Last night just after dusk I looked southwest

and saw a glint of wings, but I can't say:
hibou or heron, osprey or sharp-shinned hawk?
I only know those wings flashed and grew still.

June 30, 2022

Girl At Her Writing Desk

Susan remarked Kate's image made her think
of one of Vermeer's paintings with her scarf
and pearls lighting up the morning view.

He painted, so we're told, with cameras—
the ones they had back then were just a hole
through which light passed, projecting on a wall

an inverse image of reality
whose true perspective stayed faithful to life
so all he had to do was trace the scene.

In California, during an eclipse
I held my baseball cap above my glove
and cast six crescent suns behind the moon.

We try to do the same thing now in words:
I try to write exactly who she is
in multiple reflections accurate

to fine detail, beauty and her joy
and even pain in homage, as Vermeer
loved both the image and the lovely girl.

I Feel a Weightless Change

She always strolled through parks on my left arm
but she's switched sides lately because of pain
it takes some getting used to: to align

our pace away from what seems natural
and trying different motions around curves.
I stutter-foot it sometimes still along

our morning promenade beneath the trees.
Our daily practice: walk the labyrinth
together, pause in the heart center, touch

her hand as she half-circles me around,
together walk beneath the dawn redwood.
But crossing the stone bridge we have to go

in single file. She moves forward, steps
up huge stone blocks and fades into the pines.
I'm slower. She forgets, lost in her thought

I'm with her, half circles the island, stops—
before she goes across the bridge again—
and places her left hand on my right arm.

Koi Pond Parasols

She spends her hours at a writing desk
so I'm the one who gets the daily mail
and brings it to her study. Yesterday

brought seeds and a report card, envelopes
of almost no importance, and one slim
manila package from Petalura.

I carried it upstairs. She carefully
opened the seal revealing jewel tones
opened the scarf to show the parasols.

If you could fly above Kyoto's ponds
a sunlit summer's day, and look straight down
at women walking on the narrow paths

with each one carrying a parasol
against the bright sunlight, you'd see this scene:
almost a woodblock print on a long scarf.

She liked its gentle feel against her skin
and so today, as we walked past the ponds
she wore it to protect herself from sun.

Rilke Was Right

We lose our voices. If you want to sing
sing now. There's always something else to do
some circumstance leading to quietude:

stillness or reticence, it's all the same.
Sing now, this moment. Praise the mockingbird
outside your window in the early dawn

who woke you with a thousand joyful tunes:
a symphony perched on a single branch
rising and falling on vivacious wings.

Rilke missed weddings at his writing desk—
worried he'd lose his poem for the day:
an unimagined song lost on the wind.

"I've lost my singing voice," she said last night,
"I feel it leaving me each time I sing."
And yesterday I didn't write because:

there's always something. Sing now while you can,
sing in the darkness. Sing against the storm
before the wind takes all your breath away.

GLOSSARY

À bout de souffle: At the end of breath. French for breathless.

Baltimore: A town forty-five minutes North of our garden. Home to an aquarium, many restaurants, and Johns Hopkins University Hospital.

Baird: Scottish for 'poet.' Also, the name of my red-headed son.

Bangle: I didn't know this before I met Kate. It's like a bracelet, but it's a solid hoop. She has a whole collection, and is seldom without half a dozen.

Benadryl: It's not just for allergies. They give huge doses of it during Taxol/Keytruda chemotherapy. It made her sleepy, and made her legs shake uncontrollably.

Biopsies: They take a hollow needle, and plunge it deep into your skin. Seriously. All the way down to where the tumor is. And then they pull some of the tumor back out for analysis. A simplified version, but that's the base concept.

Bricolage: French term for a kind of cobbling together of disparate things. Building something from whatever happens to be on hand. DIY construction.

Brookside Gardens: A small botanical garden, with a conservatory, not far from our home. A place for peaceful walks in all kinds of weather. We've even made friends with some of the gardeners there. Full disclosure: I've obtained a few cuttings from their collection. I hope they never look in my greenhouse!

Capybara: A very large South American rodent who doesn't get tumors. This has led to high interest from scientists, and to the creation of interesting but completely ineffective popular folk remedies for cancer.

Carbo: A particularly brutal form of chemotherapy. Pray you can avoid it.

Chambre de Bonne: Old French for 'Maid's Room.' Now, a tiny apartment, usually in Paris, often at the highest point of a fifth-floor walkup. I lived in one near Montmartre.

Changling: Not like in the movies. This is the ability to become another. Rather like passing. Kate looks very much like an Irishwoman. But if you saw her with her Spanish choir, she could pass for Hispanic. Once, in a room full of people from India, she fit right in. She doesn't need a cloak of invisibility, she simply becomes who she's with. You don't have to believe me. If you watched it happen, you'd be amazed.

Chemo: Kate went through sixteen rounds of Chemotherapy, over a period of six months.

Coldcap: A very recently invented instrument of torture. Picture a freezer, combined with a pump, attached to a tube and a liquid-filled head skull cap. It's meant to help chemo patients retain their hair. Best case: fifty per cent of patients retain forty per cent of their hair. Worst case: it's horrible, and doesn't help at all. Kate tried, but couldn't bear it beyond one session.

Coralie Clement: A french singer with a charming voice. Her songs sound lovely and innocent, until you listen to the words. You'd never guess what lies beneath.

Cortisol: A naturally occurring hormone. During chemo, they tested her blood twice a week to track her cortisol levels.

Dawn Redwood: One of the most ancient trees in existence, dating to the Cretaceous epoch. Often called a living fossil. Every existing Dawn Redwood comes from a single specimen discovered in 1941, in the courtyard of a small shrine in a remote village in Lichuan County, Hubei Province, China. There's a particularly lovely example near the koi pond at Brookside Gardens.

Disconsolate: Inconsolable. I've succumbed to the feeling a few times.

Drug Pump: In chemotherapy, sometimes they actually pump the drugs into you. Sometimes, they simply use the pump to deliver a precise amount of drugs through an I.V. Picture a six foot metal stand, on wheels, with clear plastic bags of drugs hanging from the top, with tubes connected to four white pumps, and then to the patient. The whole thing is often referred to as a chemo tree.

"Dulce et Decorum Est": A famous poem about the horrors of World War One by Wilfred Owen. Latin, literally: it is sweet and decorous, or it is sweet and fitting. From a poem by the Roman poet Horace: 'It is sweet and decorous to die for one's country.' In Owen's ironic poem, it refers to the dying victims of a mustard gas attack.

Emploi du Temps: French for 'schedule,' or 'work schedule.'

Fleurettes: The flowering heads of a broccoli stalk.

45 R 18: The name, citing specific measurements, or a certain kind of automobile tire.

Haricots: French for 'green beans,' or 'string beans.'

Herbes de Provence: A flexible, and non-specific set of culinary herbs from the South of France. In other places, there are rigid and exact definitions of what should be included. Along the Côte d'Azur, it's whatever you happen to have in the kitchen. Cf: Salade Niçoise.

Heron: I used to love these majestic birds. Then I built koi ponds in the garden. Now, they're the arch-enemy, Moriarty to my clumsy Sherlock. They out-smart me at regular intervals.

Hibou: French for Great Horned Owl.

Keren Ann: French singer/poet/songwriter. She's not simply a popular singer, but many others do covers of her songs. Imagine a French Joni Mitchell, but much younger. You've heard her music without knowing it.

Keytruda: A new kind of chemotherapy, technically immunotherapy, also called pembro, only recently approved. Responsible for better response rates, but difficult. Kate's body couldn't take it, it almost destroyed her liver. After just a few sessions, her entire course of chemo had to be paused for several weeks, until her liver function was restored.

Knute Rockne: An American football player, best known now for wearing an uncomfortable looking leather helmet.

Koi: Japanese, short for Nishikigoi. Literally 'living jewels.' The kind of fish one sees in Japanese and Chinese garden ponds. They are the real reason I built three large ponds in the garden. Well, those, and the lotus and waterlilies.

Kyoto: One of the holy cities of Japan, celebrated for its gardens.

Labyrinth: A pattern of inlaid stones for contemplative mindful walking. Often seen in European cathedrals. Now a fixture in larger gardens. The most popular contemporary version, the Santa Rosa Labyrinth, was created in 1997 by Lea Goode-Harris. There's an excellent example at Brookside Gardens, and we walk it almost daily.

Lassitude: Weariness.

Lembert Dome: I learned rock climbing in Yosemite, not in the valley, but near Tuolumne Meadows. At the time, Lembert Dome was rated a 5.9 climb. I think the rating system has changed since then.

Life List: Bird watchers keep a list of every species of bird they've ever seen. Some go to great lengths to add one more bird to their life list.

Merlin: Cellphone app for birdwatchers, developed at Cornell Univ.

Montmartre: A neighborhood in Paris, associated with the Sacré-Coeur Basilica and the Moulin Rouge nightclub. When you hear about bohemian poets starving in a garret, they're referring to Montmartre. I lived there during my Paris days, along the Rue de Rochechouart.

N.I.H: National Institutes of Health, a huge research complex just outside Washington DC. One of our sons works at an affiliated institution.

No-Mow May: A rising trend, developed to fight the tyranny of suburban lawns, and their associated monoculture.

Oncologist: A doctor involved in the treatment of cancer. I had no idea how many kinds there are.

Paul Laurence Dunbar High: A high school near Johns Hopkins Hospital in Baltimore. Dunbar is most famous for his poem "We Wear The Mask."

Pink Sisters: On the breast cancer forums, some women refer to each other as Pink Sisters.

Port: An Implanted Port is a device, placed under the skin, to facilitate the infusion of chemo drugs. It replaces the IV needles which so often collapsed the veins in the arms of chemo patients.

Promenade: A walkway in the French city of Nice, the Promenade des Anglais, the place where the English people walk. Also, the walk itself.

Quatrième: A neighborhood on the Right Bank in Paris, home to the Notre Dame Cathedral, the Pompidou Center, and formerly the Parisian bird market.

Rachel Carson: American writer, and author of the foundational text of the environmental movement, *Silent Spring*. She lived and wrote a few hundred yards away from our home, the path along our river is named for her. She died of breast cancer.

Radiation: After her first bout of breast cancer, twenty years ago, Kate had to undergo radiation therapy. As of this writing, several more rounds are in her immediate future.

Ram Dass: Also known as Baba Ram Dass, also known as Richard Alpert. Formerly an associate of Timothy Leary. American spiritual author, best known for his book: *Remember, Be Here Now*. After being banished from Harvard, he moved to India and became the hero of the psychedelic spirituality movement.

Recette: French for recipe.

Rilke: 20th-century Austrian mystical poet, best known for his Duino Elegies and his Sonnets to Orpheus. Brilliant, eccentric, he famously missed a wedding because he didn't want to lose the poem he might write that day. It was his own daughter's wedding.

Salix: Botanical term for willow. In this case, a pussy willow. Kate's grandmother brought them into her house every spring.

Salmon: Kate's favorite food. For years, I couldn't stand the smell of its cooking, because of incidents from my childhood. When Kate got sick, I had to take over the cooking, I even had to learn how to cook salmon.

Seine: A river in Paris

Skirt Sisters: Once, we launched a book in New York City, at the famous KGB bar. Kate, always stylishly dressed, wore a lovely skirt … the same skirt the event's host, Susan Tepper, had.

Soinly: Carefully, derived from the French: Soigneusement

String of Pearls Sisterhood: Like Pink Sisters or Skirt Sisters. A friend from Europe, like Kate, always wears pearls. She sent Kate a small gift, and mentioned 'The Sisterhood of the String of Pearls.'

Surrender Dorothy: The huge white spires of the Morman Temple just outside Washington DC can be seen from the Beltway. On one of the many bridges nearby, someone wrote, in huge letters, Surrender Dorothy, a reference to *The Wizard of Oz*.

Taxol: A chemotherapy drug, derived from the yew tree.

Torii: A Japanese gate, which marks the transition from the everyday world into sacred space. Often painted red. I've acquired the wood to build one, but haven't had time yet.

Triple Negative Breast Cancer: There's not a good kind of breast cancer, but triple-negative may be the worst. A couple of decades ago, hormone-based therapies were developed for breast cancer treatment. A tumor might be ER-positive, or HER2-positive, or PR-positive. If so, it would respond to a specific kind of hormone therapy. But some tumors won't respond to any of those three, and so are labelled Triple Negative. It's a fast-growing and aggressive form of cancer. And it's the kind Kate has.

Tropicals: Tropical plants. In my garden, that mostly means Banana Trees, Elephant Ears, and Angel's Trumpets. Taken together, and planted in large numbers, those three can make the garden look like a tropical paradise.

Vireo: A small American songbird, typically having a green or gray back and yellow or white underparts.

Vermeer: Dutch painter, best known for his 'Girl with a Pearl Earring.' Now, most famous for his technique of using the 'camera obscura.' Picture a darkened room with a small hole on one wall,   through which a nearly photographic image is projected onto the opposite wall. From there, Vermeer merely had to trace the projected image onto the canvas, and then add color. This allowed for precise and absolutely authentic detail, which is also the goal of these poems.

Wisteria: The most beautiful of vines. I have nearly a dozen in the garden. Climbing up fences, rambling over the deck. I love the visual impression, Kate adores their fragrance.

Zhuangzi: Chinese Taioist philosopher and poet. Was he a man, dreaming he was a butterfly, or was he a butterfly, dreaming he was a man. I actually love him more for his argument concerning the happiness of fish, which Kate and I accidentally reproduced, two thousand years later, while driving down Route 29 in Silver Spring.

Zone Seven: The USDA divides the country into eleven gardening zones, based on how cold each gets in winter. I grew up, and learned to garden, in the paradise of Zone Ten San Diego, which never sees frost, and where one can garden every day of the year. I now live in the hellish Zone Seven, realm of blizzards and ice storms and constant frost for months of the year. Every structure needs to be built to withstand a forty-inch snowfall. Still, it could be worse: I once spent two academic years in Zone Five. Brrrr....

INDEX

Titles are semi-bold and the first lines are italicized.

ABOUT THE AUTHOR

W.F. Lantry

W.F. Lantry, a native of San Diego, is a widely published prize-winning poet and fiction writer who has been featured in poetry journals and readings nationally and internationally. He currently lives in Washington, DC.

He taught for eight years at L'Université de Nice in France, earning his License and Maîtrise in Literature, Linguistics and Translation. During this time, he won the Paris/Atlantic Young Writers Award. Boston University awarded him a Fellowship to study with Derek Walcott and George Starbuck, who together directed his thesis. There he received an M.A. in English and Creative Writing.

He holds a PhD in Literature and Creative Writing from the University of Houston where he worked with Donald Barthelme, Ed Hirsch, Mary Robison, James Robison and Adam Zagajewski. He has taught at 12 different Universities on two continents in a variety of fields, most often Literature and Rhetoric, but also in History, Library Science, World Civilizations, and Information Technology. He served as Director of Academic Technology at a national research university in Washington, DC for 15 years.

His recent honors include: Potomac Review Poetry Prize, Old Red Kimono LaNelle Daniel Prize The Linnet's Wings (Ireland) Audio Poetry Prize, Crucible Editors' Poetry Prize, Atlanta Review International Publication Prize, CutBank Patricia Goedicke Prize in Poetry, Lindberg Foundation International Poetry for Peace Prize (Israel), National Hackney Literary Award in Poetry, Comment Magazine Poetry Award.

Lantry has four times been named finalist in the Premio Mundial Fernando Rielo de Poesía Mística (Spain). In 2010, he was named runner-up for the UMB William Joiner Center Ellen LaForge Poetry Prize and the Hong Kong University Poetry Book Prize (China), he was commended for his entry in the International Hippocrates Prize for Poetry and Medicine (UK), and in Canada received Honorable Mention for the Prairie Fire Banff Centre Bliss Carman Poetry Award. In 2012, he was nominated for five Pushcart Prizes in two genres on three continents. He has given readings of his poetry in California, Texas, Connecticut, Tennessee, Massachusetts, Pennsylvania and Washington, DC. While in Nice, he participated in Interspace, a project seeking to unify Poetry, Philosophy, Music and Visual Art. As part of the Interspace project, he gave readings at the Musée Chéret and Galerie Ponchettes in Nice, Centre Pompidou in Paris, La Sapienza, Università di Roma in Italy and collaborated on a multi-media event presented at the Roccabella in Monte Carlo under the patronage of and hosted by Prince Albert.

THIS Literary Magazine selected him as Spotlight Poet, and The Tower Journal featured his work. His chapbook, *The Language of Birds*, is a lyric retelling of Attar's *Conference of the Birds*. *The Structure of Desire* (Little Red Tree Publishing) was his first full-length collection. It was followed by *The Terraced Mountain*, and will soon be joined by his forthcoming *The Book of Maps*.

He was featured in the DC area at the HearArts Spoken Word & Music Program in Rockville, the Takoma Park Poetry Reading Series and the Poetry Lab Series at The Soundry in Northern Virginia. Other recent engagements include the Kestrel Celebration at Fairmont State University, and in New York at The Poets House, the Dada Poetry Salon Series at Cornelia St. Café, the Fiele-Festa launch at KGB, and the String Poet Studio Series at the Long Island Violin Shop. His publication credits encompass print and online journals and anthologies, with his work translated into French, Arabic, Italian and Uzbek. He was the founding featured author of *Eclectica*, and new work has appeared in numerous publications in many countries including: Canada, Mexico, Scotland, France, Germany, Austria, Czech Republic, Syria, Bosnia & Herzegovina, Turkey, Israel, India, Indonesia, India, China and the UK.

CPSIA information can be obtained
at www.ICGtesting.com
Printed in the USA
BVHW020539060223
657837BV00009B/373

9 781935 656678